LOOK!
THERE'S A
KOALA

Cute, furry friends inside!

igloobooks

MEET THE KOALAS!

Say hello to your new friends! You'll find ten little koalas on every page in this fun book. Read the profiles below to learn all about their adorable personalities, then look carefully at the scenes to find each one. Flip to the back of the book to check your answers!

KATIE

BIGGEST DREAM:
To be the first koala on the moon

LOVES:
Koala-ty time with family

ALWAYS WEARS:
Red euca-lipstick

JOEY

FAVOURITE FILM:
Koala La Land

SECRET TALENT:
Magic tricks

LOVES:
Afternoon naps

SHEILA

MOST EATEN SNACK:
Eucalyptus pizza

FAVOURITE THING TO DO:
Relax by the sea

HOBBY:
Stargazing

WILLOW

BIGGEST DREAM:
To be an acrobat

MOST-LOVED ACCESSORY:
Stripy scarf

FAVOURITE HOBBY:
Skateboarding

KEITH

PERSONALITY:
Kind and funny

FAVOURITE GAME:
Chess

HOBBY:
Cheerleading

BERT

SECRET TALENT:
Tap dancing

KNOWN FOR:
Best bear hugs

FAVOURITE COLOUR:
Blue

KYLIE

MOST-LOVED ACCESSORY:
Pink glasses

FAVOURITE CHOCOLATES:
Koala-ty Street

HOBBY:
Reading novels

NIGEL

LOVES:
Hanging out with friends

FAVOURITE DRINK:
Coca Koala

SECRET TALENT:
Rapping

HOPE

SECRET TALENT:
Playing the drums

BIGGEST GOAL:
To be a koala-fied pilot

KNOWN FOR:
Always being helpful

BASIL

FAVOURITE SWEETS:
Gummy bears

PERSONALITY:
Sweet and gentle

LOVES:
Climbing

CHOCOLATE HEAVEN

Yum! Look at all that delicious chocolate!
Ten koalas are exploring. Can you see them?

CAN YOU SPOT THE GREEN SWEET?

SUNNY SEASIDE

The beach is so busy today! Where are the koalas splashing, playing and relaxing?

T-DDI-- AND T-Y-

The koalas are playing hide-and-seek in the toy shop.
Peek between the cuddly toys to find them all!

CAN YOU SPOT THE ORANGE SHIELD?

P-RFECT PICNIC

The koalas are enjoying koala-ty time together at the park. Do you think you can spot all ten?

CAN YOU SPOT THE ONLY RED ICE LOLLY?

KOALA CANDYLAND

There's so much to explore in this sugary scene!
Where are all ten playful koalas hiding?

CAN YOU SPOT THE YELLOW CANDY CANE?

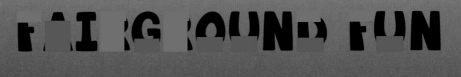

FAIRGROUND FUN

Ten koalas are having fun at the fair. Look closely
at the crowds and rides to spot each one.

SKATING STARS

The koalas love going ice skating! They whirl and twirl across the rink. Can you find them all?

CAN YOU SPOT THE BRIGHT PINK PRESENT?

SUPER SPORTS

Ready, steady... race! It's time for lots of sports day games!
There are ten koalas joining in, but can you see where?

CAN YOU SPOT THE SILVER AND PINK MEDAL?

DEEP-SEA DIVE

There's so much to spot under the splashing waves!
Look closely to find all ten koalas exploring.

CAN YOU SPOT THE ONLY PINK TURTLE?

AWESOME ALIENS

3... 2... 1... BLAST OFF! The koalas meet lots of cool aliens in space. Can you see all ten koalas floating around?

CAN YOU SPOT THE SPACE PIZZA?

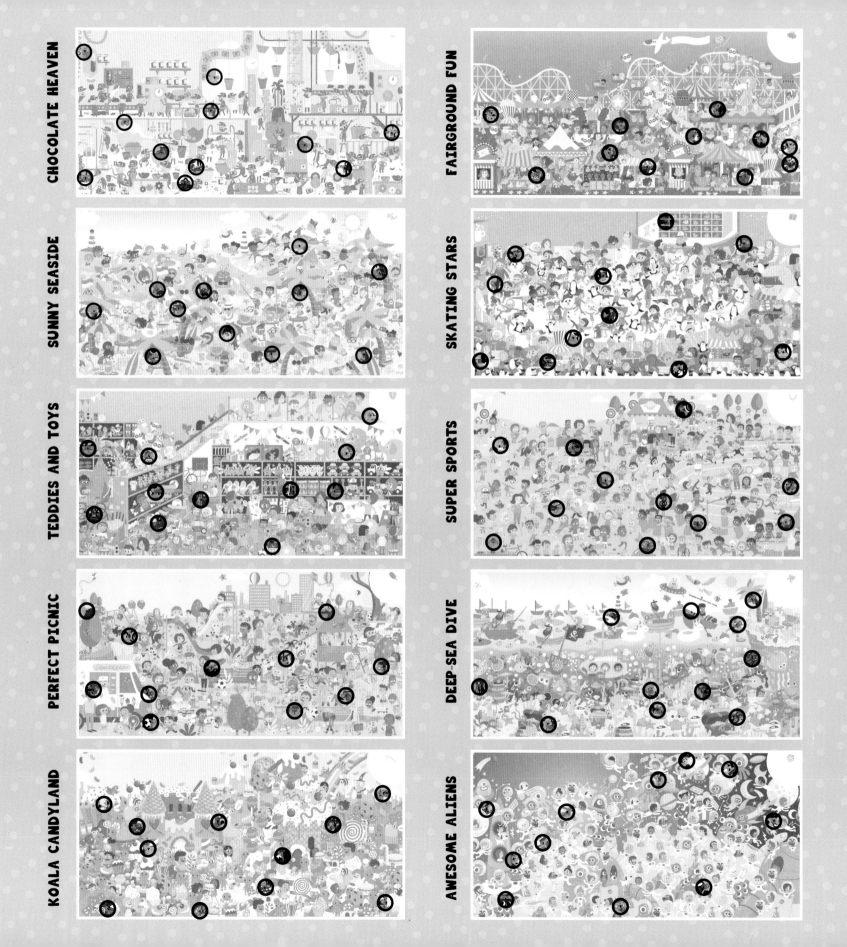

CHOCOLATE HEAVEN

FAIRGROUND FUN

SUNNY SEASIDE

SKATING STARS

TEDDIES AND TOYS

SUPER SPORTS

PERFECT PICNIC

DEEP-SEA DIVE

KOALA CANDYLAND

AWESOME ALIENS